I0807928

SPIRITUAL SYNERGY

A Ladies' Manual to Becoming Spiritually Fit

Tammy Carpenter

WESTBOW
P R E S S®
A DIVISION OF THOMAS NELSON
& ZONDERVAN

WestBow Press books may be ordered through booksellers or by contacting:

WestBow Press
A Division of Thomas Nelson & Zondervan
1663 Liberty Drive
Bloomington, IN 47403
www.westbowpress.com
1 (866) 928-1240

Unless otherwise noted, Scripture taken from the New King James Version, Copyright © 1982 by Thomas Nelson, Inc. Used by permission. All rights reserved.

Scripture quotations marked "NLT" are taken from the Holy Bible, New Living Translation, Copyright © 1996. Used by permission of Tyndale House Publishers, Inc. Wheaton, Illinois 60189. All rights reserved.

Scripture quotations marked "KJV" are taken from the Holy Bible, King James Version, Cambridge, 1769.

ISBN: 978-1-4908-9823-0 (sc)
ISBN: 978-1-4908-9824-7 (e)

Print information available on the last page.

WestBow Press rev. date: 12/21/2015

Spiritual Synergy

"Spiritual Synergy is a straightforward, challenging, and encouraging book that will have you examining your spiritual life. How much more important it is for us to be spiritually fit than physically fit! These "workouts" will be time well spent in God's word." "Having been in several Bible studies taught by Tammy Carpenter, I can assure you of her genuine faith and her desire to encourage women in their spiritual walk. Her wisdom and knowledge are inspiring, and she communicates Biblical truths in a way we ladies relate to."

Julie Neal, Pastor's Wife, Christ Fellowship Church, Palm Beach Gardens, Florida

"God often uses the natural world to illustrate spiritual principles. Physical health and fitness is one of the pictures He uses to speak to us about maximizing our spiritual health in order to fulfill His destiny for us. Tammy helps us take a good look at where we need to lose spiritual weight we may have picked up, often without realizing it. She then identifies key areas where we can work together with the Holy Spirit to build ourselves up to be at our very best to love and serve Him! Each section is short, simple and packed with scripture . . . be sure to take time to read, pray and apply what you discover in the questions that follow!"

Lisa Orvis, Director, Educating For Life, Youth With A Mission, Hawaii

"Your in for the workout of your life with this manual: in the down to earth tone of a caring coach, Carpenter outlines a scriptural exercise regimen for those who need to shed the spiritual weight of sin or put on some muscle of spiritual maturity."

Wendy Wharton, MA, LPCMH,
Life Counseling Center, Delaware Physical Ed.
Teacher & Middle School Track & Field Coach

I dedicate this study to my Lord Jesus Christ to use for His service. It is through Christ and for His glory that I have written this study guide.

I also dedicate this book to my only daughter, Jessica Renee. May you soar with eagles as you continue to walk steadfastly with our Savior.

CONTENTS

PREFACE

The birthing process of *Spiritual Synergy* was much longer than the nine months of a physical pregnancy. The principles written through out *Spiritual Synergy* are tried and true from my own life experiences.

My spiritual journey began at the young age of five when I accepted Christ. I spent the majority of my childhood a few miles from my father's college, Liberty Bible College in Pensacola, Florida. It was at Liberty, in this Bible belt community, that I listened to Bible scholars from all over the world speak.

In 1992, I married my husband, James, and settled down on his family farm. A farm located 1100 miles from my friends, my church, my college groups, and the beaches of Pensacola. I was confident about moving to Delaware. I was in love and I had always envisioned raising my children on a farm. It was during those first eight years of marriage, alone, tired, and pregnant four times, that the application of *Spiritual Synergy* was birthed. I wept, studied, prayed, fasted, and sought the Lord – not always in that order. I was struggling for significance. Where was the abundant life in Jesus Christ I had learned about? Where was the peace beyond understanding? I didn't see it in my life or my community. I was miles from the Bible belt, that was for sure.

After attending a Christian women's conference, I had a compelling desire to journal the Biblical principles I had applied to my life during those lonely years. Each major point became a chapter of this book.

Writing a book was completely out of my comfort zone. However, the Holy Spirit began to guide me. There are multitudes of women, just like me who are searching for significance. They too needed to find biblical solutions to everyday problems. I knew I needed to provide a workbook with a simple format that would take women on all different spiritual levels to a higher and deeper relationship with their God. I wanted to start with my daughter.

When I thought about the presentation theme, it seemed that everywhere I looked, I saw or heard something about exercise. Weight, diet, or fitness was mentioned almost every time I was with a group of women. I had spent my entire life battling the bulge and I grew tired of hearing the words, "big boned". I would exercise hard to fit in with the small, slender, women. Negative lies would surface in my thoughts; " If I was smaller, lighter, and prettier, I would be experiencing that abundant life in Christ." I would then exercise and diet even more, leaving me emotionally, spiritually, and physically exhausted. I noticed that God often uses the physical to define the spiritual. It was clear to me; exercise would be the synergy I'd use in my book.

I converted the principle points into a spiritual fitness workout manual. Each chapter either focuses on losing the weight that is damaging your spirit or gaining the muscle to strengthen your spiritual being. I even added a Detox to boost the cleansing process of your heart (a quick Biblical remedy to raise your spiritual temperature).

I pray this workbook will guide you through Biblical solutions to find your true significance in Jesus Christ. You, the reader are beautiful, loved and treasured by you Heavenly Father. He has a plan and a purpose for you. Begin studying today, and allow God to define your destiny. I appreciate your interest in my story and love you as my sister in Christ.

Be blessed, Tammy

INTRODUCTION

Caution: This workout is not for the fainthearted. Consult our Creator. This manual is for the weak that they become strong.

Ladies, why is it that we put so much emphasis on working out our physical body and neglect our spiritual being? Millions of women exercise five to seven times a week. We are consistently trying to tone and recondition our aging bodies. I agree that taking care of your physical body—your "temple"—is not only a priority but also a requirement.

In this book I'm not going to focus on the physical, because our society is flooded with good nutritional and exercise books to help even the beginner. Instead, I want to encourage you to transform your spiritual being into the image of Christ. You must understand that whatever you do with your physical body affects your spiritual being. My prayer for you is that you take the time through the Word of God to tone and recondition your spiritual being. The results will be life changing. Christ tells us that He gives us life and life more abundantly.

To become spiritually fit we must remove those things from our lives that hinder spiritual progress. To raise our spiritual temperature is like raising our heart rate to burn more calories. Join me in allowing God to burn out those areas in our lives that are not up to His biblical standards.

Paul tells us to examine our own faith (2 Corinthians 13:5). Each chapter in this book will focus on a different area that could cause blockage or allow growth in our spiritual progress. Please pray regarding each subject so that in your life, these areas glorify God.

THINGS TO CONSIDER

1) What does Paul mean when he says that "our bodies are the temple of the Holy Spirit" in 1 Corinthians 6:19?

2) Read Romans 12:2. Why do we need to transform our minds?

3) According to John 10:10, what was Christ's purpose in coming?

4) According to 1 Corinthians 6:20, as believers, who owns us and what is our purpose?

5) Are we to question our own faith? Read 2 Corinthians 13:5.

CRISIS INTERVENTION DETOX DIET

Has the weight of the world got you spinning out of control? This is a quick cheat sheet to get you on your way.

1) Pray without ceasing. (1 Thessalonians 5:17)
2) Transform your mind by the reading of the Word. (Romans 12:2)
3) Fast, if health allows. (Mark 9:29; 1 Corinthians 7:5)
4) Play Christian music. (Isaiah 61:3)
5) Sing and dance to the Lord, even if you don't feel like it. (Psalm 149:3)
6) Play Christian messages in your home. (Proverbs 19:20)
7) Be quiet before the Lord. (Psalm 46:10)
8) Read Scripture promises aloud in your home. (2 Corinthians 4:13-14)
9) Post Scripture around your home, workplace, and car. (Deuteronomy 11:20)
10) Take every thought captive. (2 Corinthians 10:5)
11) Continually thank God. (Hebrews 13:15)
12) Stick to the Ten Commandments no matter what. (John 14:15)

WEIGHT #1

A HEAVY HEART

Before you begin any exercise program, your physician wants to listen to your heart. The same is true with the Great Physician, our Creator. God wants to know: How's your heart? Is it carrying unnecessary weight? How's the blood flow? Is the blood of Jesus being pumped through your veins?

The book of Proverbs elevates our heart above everything else. Proverbs 4:23 states, "Above all else, guard your heart, for it is the wellspring of life" (NLT). We must protect our hearts every day. To become spiritually fit, we must begin by exercising our source (wellspring), which is our heart.

The first step to becoming spiritual fit is accepting Jesus as Lord of your life. He is knocking at your heart's door, patiently and eagerly, waiting for you to allow Him in. Romans 10:9 says, "If you confess with your mouth the Lord Jesus and believe in your heart that God has raised him from the dead, you will be saved." Confession is a heart to heart conversation with God – known as prayer. Relinquish your control by acknowledging that you have sinned and ask God for forgiveness. Express your desire to have Jesus as Lord of your life, believing that his death and resurrection will reconcile you with your Creator. Then close this and every prayer "In Jesus' name". At this point, you may begin your journey to disciple your spiritual being. No need to wait. You have received the treasured gift of salvation. In this lesson we will learn how to guard your heart from heaviness caused by the burdens of this world.

The first weight we are going to lose is a heavy heart. Mary, mother of Jesus, is a beautiful example of a woman who lived weightless by guarding her heart. Mary was honored above all women. An angel appeared to her, and the shepherds came and told her that her baby was the Savior, Christ the Lord. Wow! What a great post for Facebook. She could have texted everyone in her contacts. Yet, Luke 2:19 says, "Mary kept all these sayings, pondering them in her heart." When the angel also appeared later to her husband, Joseph, he was able to confirm what God placed in her.

Many times women add weight by revealing the secret places of their heart to those it does not concern. Just as Mary conceived and gave birth to our Savior, you, too, have a calling. Ponder that calling in your heart. Allow it to be conceived through prayer and meditation on

God's Word. Study the Word of God to show yourself approved.

In God's due season, your calling will be birthed through His sovereignty. God will bring the right husband, wise men, and shepherds to come forth to announce and bring purpose to your life. God is the hero of your story. Your heart will be weightless, as He receives all the glory. We are to ponder things in our heart, but this does not include our salvation. We are daughters of the Most High God, and that is what we publicly proclaim. That should be our post on Facebook. Let His story be your testimony.

THINGS TO CONSIDER

1) According to Proverbs 15:13, what role does the heart play in our personality?

2) Read Matthew 7:6. What are your pearls, and who would be the swine? When you protect your pearls, are you protecting your heart?

3) Instead of proclaiming the desires of our hearts, what should we do? (Psalm 37:4)

4) What does Jesus say His purpose is for you as a believer? (John 10:10)

5) There are different seasons in our lives: a time to conceive and a time to birth. What can we expect if we do not grow weary? (Galatians 6:9)

6) List those things in your heart that God has given you to guard, such as your marriage, your family, your beliefs, your vision, your goals, your friendships, your country, etc.

7) Pray to God for His revelation in guarding these things. Ask God to forgive you for the things He has given you stewardship of and you have not guarded.

LIFE EXERCISED

The day I accepted Jesus as my Savior has stayed with me always; I remember it vividly. I was only five years old when my parents accepted Christ as adults. Even at that young age I was able to notice a significant change in the behaviors and the atmosphere of our home. We began going to church and studying the Bible together through family devotions.

There was still something missing from my life. Night was my greatest fear. I'd awaken from haunting nightmares only to have shadows creep on my walls—there was no escaping these terrors. Every night I felt as if I'd been brushed by the Devil himself! I wanted what my parents and older brother had received; I wanted this Jesus to give me victory, peace, and sleep!

I can still see my mom sitting at her sewing machine, busily working under the glow of the desk lamp. "Mom," I said as she turned toward me, "I want to get saved." She then began sharing the same thing I just shared with you. I stood there by the sewing table and repented of my sins, and Jesus entered my heart.

Immediately the shadows and nightmares left my bedroom as the holy Light of the World came into me. From that moment forward I have had a strong passion to share with others this Jesus who changed my life. In kindergarten I would place Christian tracts in my classmates' cubbies— even leading a few of my peers to Christ during recess. That fire inside has continued to this day, leading me to write this book and share the good news.

who is on your back?

WEIGHT #2

NEGATIVE PEOPLE

Isn't it ironic that human beings—one of God's greatest creations, created to bring Him pleasure (Revelation 4:11)—can also bring the most grief? We need other people in our lives, and the Bible tells us not to forsake the fellowship of the saints (Hebrews 10:25). Even though we have this need, sometimes relationships can be burdensome.

The important question to consider is this: How do we become spiritually fit and still fellowship with other people? Boundaries are essential. While living in this world, we are not to conform to it (Romans 12:2). The Bible is full of

God's standards in any relationship. When we relate to people in the manner God wants us to, the weight is lifted.

If people are weighing you down, maybe shedding emotional pounds in the people department is your answer. One way to do this is to evaluate your current friendships. Are they producing good fruit? Do your relationships encourage you to become more like Christ?

Consider each of these items regarding the individuals in your life. Do they help you to . . .

- love and submit to your spouse (Ephesians 5:22)?
- nurture and guide your children (Proverbs 22:6)? Would you send your children to these individuals for advice (Proverbs12:26)?
- think on those things that are holy, pure, and true (Philippians 4:8)?

If your friendships and relationships are not leading you to Christ, then you are carrying a huge weight, and you are yoked to those people. Jesus tells us to carry His yoke, which is easy (Matthew 11:30). Give these people to the Lord. Be prepared for emptiness, because you have trained yourself to carry all this drama, and the quiet peace may seem abnormal at first.

As you train yourself to share Christ's yoke, you will find this peace and quiet a sacred blessing. Later in this manual we will add the weight of wisdom and discernment to our spiritual being. This will prevent us from being entangled in the weight of others.

THINGS TO CONSIDER

1) What type of people should we not agree with?
   (Proverbs 1:10-19; 2 Timothy 2:23)

2) To whom should we not be unequally yoked?
   (2 Corinthians 6:14)

3) When do true friends show their love? (Proverbs 17:17)

4) Who are the weightless people? (Psalm 15:1-5)

5) Should we shed a husband if he is weighing us down?
   (1 Corinthians 7:39)

LIFE EXERCISED

A teachable moment for myself was when a dear friend of mine was leaving to serve in the military overseas. She was leaving four children home with her husband and asked if she could put my cell phone number in her oldest daughter's contacts. She told me how she was unsure of what the future may hold, but she was sure that she wanted her girls to be able to contact someone who would give them godly advice.

I was honored. At the same time, I began to question who my children would call in my absence. I shared with my kids those who I thought would give them godly advice and support them in the purposes God has for them. It is very important who you surround yourself with as a parent. Not only will those people influence you, but even more so your children.

WEIGHT #3

UNDISCIPLINED

Discipline is the key to a successful fitness program. Many personal trainers will coach you to be consistent every day, no matter how easy or intense the workout. So it is with your spiritual health. God has given each of us a free personal trainer: the Holy Spirit, our Counselor (John 14: 26 NLT). He will never leave us or forsake us (John 14:16).

What a promise! The more we exercise with the Holy Spirit, the greater the reward. Discipline is needed for every exercise. As with any fitness program, participants are encouraged when they see results. God has promised results when we exercise in His Word. His Word will not return void (Isaiah 55:11). There will always be results. We as believers must be consistent to gain victory. We cannot read the Bible a couple of times or say a few prayers and expect a close encounter. A disciplined life will yield results.

Discipline will set you on a strict regimen of exercise that transforms your mind, heart, and soul into the character of Christ. Paul writes about this perseverance in his letter to the Corinthians (1 Corinthians 9:25-27). Paul compares this spiritual training to that of an athlete preparing to win a race or trophy. Just as an athlete removes any hindrance to pursuing his or her goal, we must have that same attitude with our spiritual health. We must focus on the goal: eternity with our Lord Jesus Christ. Do not become distracted.

The goal of everything we say or do must be to bring us closer to our Savior. Each day, take time to pray and meditate on God's Word. Become enthralled with being in God's presence. The Holy Spirit can be your personal trainer, and spending time with Him should give you energy. Nothing feeds a heart and soul more than the presence of the holy, living God.

Start out with a few minutes daily. Gradually, it will become an all-day activity. Whether we are in the car, home, workplace, church, or grocery store, we should seek His presence. Living a disciplined life is essential to accepting the fullness of Christ in our lives.

THINGS TO CONSIDER

1) What is the dictionary definition of *discipline*?

2) How are we to run this race as believers? Who is the leader of the race? (Hebrews 12:1-2)

3) What type of training are believers supposed to pursue? (1 Timothy 4:7-8)

4) In what exercises are we to be disciplined as believers? (Romans 12:1-2; Ephesians 2:10; 6:18; Philippians 4:11)

LIFE EXERCISED

Staying focused is essential to seeing results.

I can recall way back to when my four children were crawling, crying, hungry, and dirty—all at the same time! They needed so much constant attention. There were days I felt my life was completely drained from my body. To keep on, I stayed confident that the joy of the Lord is my strength. I disciplined myself, no matter how difficult at times, to spend at least ten minutes a day studying God's Word—many times in my bathroom while trying to take a quick breather!

Those ten precious minutes became my lifeline as the Holy Spirit always led me to the perfect Bible passage to strengthen my day. Then I would end my prayer hearing the tiny fist of one of my kids knocking on the door: "Mommy, I need you!" And I was ready, prepared, and focused. I had my second wind.

WEIGHT #4

ROTTEN FRUIT

Raising our spiritual temperature is a combination of many things. We must surrender every area of our life to an all-knowing God. There is nothing in our lives that we can keep hidden from our heavenly Father. Sometimes we try to conceal or camouflage body fat under our clothing, but we know it is still there. The Bible refers to these concealed areas of our lives as "bad fruit" and tells us to regularly prune them (John 15:2). This rotten fruit will weigh down our body, soul, and spirit to the point of crippling us and making us unable to receive the full reward God has for us (Romans 7:5).

To remove this unwanted weight from our spiritual being, we must begin with prayer. Surrender yourself to the Creator, allowing the Holy Spirit to counsel you. The Holy Spirit will guide you in examining your motives in everything you do. Some activities may be easy to see as extra weight. Other activities may be disguised behind good deeds.

Consider where you are in life (single, married, divorced, a mother), and analyze the effect of your actions on those areas for which you are responsible. An example of an unwanted weight activity would be if a wife/mother routinely spent her evenings drinking at a bar. The decaying fruit would be evident, not only in her own life but also in the lives of her husband and children. A more subtle example of a weight-bearing activity would be if a wife/mother routinely spent her evenings volunteering at a church instead of tending to or loving her family.

As women, we do have God-given responsibilities. When we stray from these duties, we will bear rotten fruit. The decay may be in our marriage, relationships, eating habits, and even our children. (I'm not at all implying that the father's role does not play an important part in the fruit of the children—it does.)

This workbook is dedicated to women, and each of us will stand before God alone. Our husbands, parents, pastor, or friends will not be there to defend our motives. First Corinthians 3:13-15 says that those fruits that we spent so much time cultivating in our lives that were not our responsibility will reap no reward, no gain at all—they were a complete waste of time. How's that for a workout?

I encourage you to pursue the reward of the faithful servant (Matthew 25:21). Drop the weight of any activity that is not your God-given responsibility. This will raise your spiritual temperature and great will be your reward. Later, we will examine the fruit of the Spirit that bears good fruit.

THINGS TO CONSIDER

1) Is God really all-knowing? (Isaiah 40:10-12)

2) What is the only way we can bear much fruit? (John 15:5-8)

3) When we "abide" in Christ, what type of fruit will we bear? (John 15:5)

4) What are the fruits of the Spirit? (Galatians 5:22-23)

5) List the rotten fruit described as wickedness in these two references: Romans 1:29-32 and 2 Corinthians 12:20.

6) What are the God-given responsibilities of a Christian woman? (1 Timothy 5:14; Titus 2:3-5)

LIFE EXERCISED

Upon graduation from college, I was offered a staff position at my local Pregnancy Care Center. What a great experience, watching first hand, women's lives being impacted by the love of Christ during their pregnancy. It was exhilarating! Just as the PCC was growing, so was my own family. When my first child, Jessica, arrived I resigned to become a stay-at-home mom. Fourteen months later my second child, JT, arrived. Even though I had resigned from my staff position, I still volunteered once a week as a lay counselor. My vision was to continue counseling once a week forever. Soon, I realized the good fruit I was bearing at the PCC was sowing seeds of rotten fruit at home. As a young mom, I was 1100 miles from my hometown in Florida. I had not yet built a support system to care for my babies while I was ministering. I was putting a tremendous strain on my family, especially my husband who was working long hours on his farm. It was a special treat for our kids to take a ride with daddy in the tractor, but all day was difficult on everyone. Slowly, the rotten fruit began to grow. I realized that my first calling is to my husband and children. My ministry is at home with my family. Once that is in balance, I can minister to others. Fortunately, over a decade later, I have been able to return to the Pregnancy Care Center ministry, as a Board Member for a local PCC. Volunteering will always be available, raising your children will not. Be sure that you're bearing good fruit in the right season.

WEIGHT #5

DISOBEDIENCE

As with any exercise program, optimum results are obtained by strictly following detailed guidelines. Many times we watch a diet or exercise commercial, and on the bottom of the screen there is a disclaimer: *These results are not typical from using this product.* A strict diet and daily exercise were followed. Simply said, this was the true key to success.

A similar requirement is essential for our spiritual being. One requirement is obedience. Obeying God's Word (through confession and true repentance) is the exercise for burning off the weight of disobedience. Disobeying God allows consequences into our lives that will weigh down our spiritual walk. We want to stay free of that weight. Jesus says in John 14:15, "If you love me keep my commandments." We want to position our lives on the track of loving God. It will become natural to obey Him as we walk in our love for Him. He has already given us the diet plan for a healthy life.

God's Word is our owner's manual handed to us directly from our Creator. We can rely solely upon God's Word for complete directions. Before Jesus lived on earth, humanity relied on the Ten Commandments as a list of what was right and wrong. When Jesus lived among us, He gave us a new perspective on the Ten Commandments. He summed them all up into two commandments, the first being, "You shall love the Lord your God with all your heart, with all your soul, and with all your mind." The second one is, "You shall love your neighbor as yourself" (Matthew 22:37-40). When we obey these two commandments, we will completely fulfill all the others listed in the Bible.

THINGS TO CONSIDER

1) List and briefly define each of the Ten Commandments. (Exodus 20:1-17)

2) Go back to each of your answers for question 1 and explain how you can adequately fulfill the original commandments by walking out your love for God. (Matthew 5:21-48)

3) What is God's promise to us when we obey Him?
(Jeremiah 7:23; Hebrews 5:9)

4) What is the result of disobedience?
(2 Thessalonians 1:8-9)

LIFE EXERCISED

By nature, I am a rule follower, so for me to get completely off the straight-and-narrow path would be out of character. Yet, I still have to be very careful committing admissible sins (the ones that are not noticeable). When my brother passed away at the young age of thirty-nine from cancer, I realized I needed to ask God for forgiveness. The void left by his death revealed I had put trust into my relationship with my brother that should have been given to God.

In John's passing, I was empty and had no hope for the future; my outlook on life took a drastic change. John was my big brother, and I knew that if anything were to ever go wrong, he would have my back and take care of it. When he was gone, I felt lost and alone—then I was convicted.

I immediately asked Christ for forgiveness and trusted Him with a new vigor. What a peace I experienced! Even though I miss my brother, and there are times I tear up when I see a picture, I am able to smile. I still have the opportunity to love John's widow and their wonderful son. They are such treasures in my life, and I feel blessed. I know God will take care of us all.

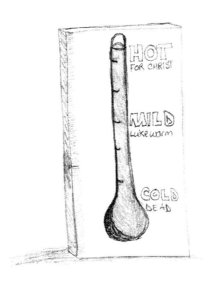

WEIGHT #6

LUKEWARMNESS

Lukewarmness is a very deceitful weight. Many people who claim to be Christians don't even realize that it is their own lukewarmness that weighs them down. These people are deceived into believing that their limited commitment to Christ will give them the same result as a fully surrendered believer. Just as exercise is a daily commitment, being a Christian is daily carrying the cross of Christ (Luke 9:23-26).

A person can show up at the gym with the latest workout apparel a few times a year. This may give the impression to those who witness their appearance that they are dedicated to becoming "fit." Yet to their personal trainer it means nothing. Unfortunately, a few visits to the gym annually will not produce results.

The same dynamic happens in our spiritual being if we do not have that daily relationship with our precious Savior. Many people become Christian CEOs and only attend church on Christmas, Easter, and other organized holidays thinking they have accomplished their Christian "duties." This lack of involvement will not produce an intimate relationship with God. Our spiritual temperature will be lukewarm.

This lukewarmness is neither hot nor cold, and it is a very dangerous place for our spiritual being (Revelation 3:15-16). As with any exercise routine, we must surrender our heart to our Lord Jesus daily. This will drop the weight of lukewarmness, allowing our spiritual temperature to rise.

THINGS TO CONSIDER

1) How do we surrender our lives totally to Jesus Christ? And what do we gain by doing so? (Mark 8:34-35)

2) Can a person mimic a believer without being totally surrendered? What is the end result? (Matthew 7:21-23; Jude 1:4-5)

3) What happens when a believer helps another believer surrender totally to Christ? (James 5:19-20)

4) What is the reward for those who stay surrendered to Christ? (2 Timothy 4:7-8)

5) How does Christ feel about lukewarmness? What is His goal for mankind? (Revelation 3:15-21)

LIFE EXERCISED

I have always appreciated Keith Green's analogy, "Going to church doesn't make you a Christian any more than going to McDonald's makes you a hamburger!" I was blessed to worship with Keith's widow during my time at Last Day's Ministries with Youth with a Mission (YWAM). So live out your faith! Don't simply go through the motions.

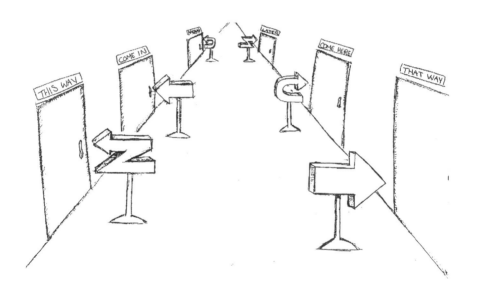

WEIGHT #7

NO VISION

A crucial step to any positive development in our lives is having a vision or vivid plan for our future. If we aim for nothing, that is what we will hit in life. To continue any exercise routine, one must know the steps and ultimately the desired outcome. Many times a coach will write down a person's individual goals for what they would like to accomplish over a course of time such as strength, energy level, weight loss, and endurance. It is the same for our spiritual health.

Fortunately, our heavenly Father already has an individual plan for each of us (Jeremiah 29:11 NLT). As we seek Him, He will reveal more of this plan to us daily. We must understand that the reverse is also true. The Bible says, "Where there is no vision, the people perish" (Proverbs 29:18 KJV) This is not only a warning, but "lack of vision" is a heavy weight to bear. Not knowing what direction to take keeps a person buried in their past, unable to move forward. Paul tells us that he presses on toward the goal of the high calling (Philippians 3:14). When you allow your heart, mind, and soul to grab hold of the vision, it will bring hope.

When the desire of hope comes, it is a tree of life (Proverbs 13:12). Hope replaces the weight of aimless living. Hope accepts the vision God has for you and incorporates it into your daily living.

THINGS TO CONSIDER

1) According to Jeremiah 29:11, what is God's plan for us?

2) What is the result of living life aimlessly?
   (Proverbs 29:18; Hosea 4:6)

3) As a believer, what should your focus be on?
   (Philippians 3:13-14)

4) How does hope inspire our vision and purpose in life?
   (Proverbs 13:12; Romans 5:5; 8:24-25; 12:12; 15:13)

5) Write down the vision God has given you, including steps and goals. List every area of your life: single, wife, mother, employee, employer, sister, aunt, grandmother, community member, and any other hat you may wear. Allow God to gently speak into each area of your life and give you a vision of His purposes. (Habakkuk 2:2)

LIFE EXERCISED

I found that goals are accomplished more quickly when they are written down. Even for daily errands, I will write a list in the most efficient order so that they can be completed as to optimize time. I've heard many writers say they keep a tablet beside their bed for those "light bulb" moments.

This manual was in my heart and mind for quite some time, but it did not become a goal until I began writing down the topics. Thank you for helping me accomplish my vision for this book, allowing me to encourage women like yourself.

WEIGHT #8

SUPERSPIRITUAL

We live in a society where everything is better supersized, from our food to our entertainment. Superheroes rule the earth with supernatural powers. It is no wonder this same mentality has crept into the body of Christ. These people identify themselves as Superspiritual Saints. Everyone should appreciate them since (they believe) the church would be devastated without them.

Sounds like an exercise we should try to achieve. Yet, only the opposite is true. This contradicts the teachings of the Holy Scripture. The Bible says the first shall be last (Mark 10:31). The Super Saint is in for a rude awakening. Luke 18:14 says, "Whoever exalts himself will be humbled." Pride is a crushing weight—a weight that when lifted, falls back down upon an unprepared individual, causing injury. When pride comes, then comes shame (Proverbs 11:2).

How do we escape the injury of pride? We should not attempt to do things in our own strength. God has given us a spotter, the Holy Spirit. He will counsel us through Scripture. Jesus Himself advises us on tangible ways to stay humble. In fact, He tells us when we are out in public to not sit down in the best place at a table. Instead, take the lowest place. Then those who have invited you can offer you a more prominent position (Luke 14:8-11). When a woman exalts herself, she eclipses the glory of God. This allows the weight of pride to destroy her life. Ultimately, all glory is due to our Creator (Isaiah 2:11).

THINGS TO CONSIDER

1) How can those who will inherit the kingdom of God serve the least of the brethren today? (Matthew 25:40)

2) Read Isaiah 3:16-26.

   a) List the characteristics of a prideful, haughty woman.

b) What will be the results of these prideful actions?

3) Who are the blessed that will inherit the earth and eternal life? (Matthew 5:2-11)

LIFE EXERCISED

Have you ever wanted to join a Ladies Bible Study, only to find out you're not welcome? You watch women praising God, sharing the Word, and filling positions in the church, yet they don't want to be bothered with some frumpy woman like yourself? I hear these disturbing stories from Christian women, young and old, regularly. All have fallen victim to Mrs. Super Spiritual. Somehow super sizing religion has allowed these monstrous women to crush the hearts of their sisters. With crushed hearts in hand many have left the church for good. Instagram/Facebook envy begins with seeing postings of Christian women having a Ladies night out, bible study, or attending a Women's conference without inviting you. It stings. It's hard to watch sister's in Christ being snubbed, alienated, criticized, and embarrassed within the walls of the church. It makes your flesh cry out to give these Mrs. S.S. a piece of their own medicine. I imagine these women long to take vengeance in their own hand. If this is happening to you remind yourself of Isaiah 3:16-26. Obviously their moment of glory will fade ever so quickly. My heart grieves for these Mrs. S.S. Their end reward is not worth the fleeting popularity. Keep your spirituality in check. God will never allow Super Spirituality to eclipse His glory.

*Duck-tape can fix more than objects

WEIGHT #9

GOSSIP

Working out our flesh and working in the Holy Spirit is a daily endeavor. It involves staying consistent and daily feeding our spiritual man the living bread (John 6:51). When incorporating a full-body workout, each muscle carries its own weight. So it is with one of the smallest muscles, the tongue (James 3:5). This small muscle, when worked in the wrong direction, can cause havoc to one's soul. Instead of being small and insignificant, it becomes a muscle on steroids, enlarging itself to the point where no other part of an individual is even noticed.

Sadly enough, many women feel empowered by this workout. Being the first to know of a difficult situation gives them an illusion of strength. They spread the gossip by working out their tongue to gain popularity. Everyone wants to know their wealth of information. For a season, they are the life of the party, a hit on the Internet, and their phone is constantly ringing (Hebrews 11:25). Even in the religious community, this behavior is exalted. Ladies will comment on the new information with, "We must pray for her." Unfortunately, this is a destructive weight of gossip, backbiting, and careless talk (Proverbs 11:11-13).

To remove this weight from destroying our lives, we must bridle our tongue. In James 3:2-5, he likens the tongue to the bit in a horse's mouth and a rudder on a ship. Our tongue will decide the direction our lives will take. Peter encourages us to "refrain our tongue from evil and our lips from speaking deceit." He also reminds us that "the face of the Lord is against those who do evil" (1 Peter 3:10-12). This would be a terrible weight to carry through life. Let's decide to keep our tongue bridled and walk in righteousness.

THINGS TO CONSIDER

1) What happens if we do not bridle our tongues?
   (James 1:26)

2) What does the Bible tell us about careless talk?
   (Ecclesiastes 5:2; Matthew 12:36-37)

3) Is there any wisdom in being quiet? (Proverbs17:27-28)

4) How can we take a "dog by the ears"? (Proverbs 26:17)

5) According to Titus 2:3-5, how are women to conduct themselves?

LIFE EXERCISED

Oh boy, we've all been there, gossip. Somehow, when it's masked with the title of "prayer request", it seems okay. I too, have fallen in this trap. To stop myself, I ask this question, "Is this my story to tell? Will there be something positive from me sharing?"

With today's technology, we have to be extremely cautious with sharing. One touch of a button and our message is forwarded to all of our contacts. It's a very easy mistake, to send a private message to the masses. Our mind (thoughts) directs our actions. So, if you're sharing someone's personal story, there is a great chance that you will send it directly to the person you are talking about instead of for who it is intended. A betrayal this large could end a relationship. That's why God condemns gossip. Thanks be to God for forgiveness. Make a choice to keep names out of emails, text messages, etc. Even if you think someone would appreciate a prayer request being sent out, always request permission first.

LIFTING WEIGHT #1

FRUIT OF THE SPIRIT

Up to this chapter in our manual, we have been dropping weight. In a majority of exercise routines, this is the ultimate outcome: the loss of weight. Yet to raise our spiritual temperature, we now need to add the essential items that will replace our prior bad habits. We've crucified our flesh, and we now take on our new creation (Galatians 5:24).

It is common knowledge that when there is weight loss, there must be muscle gain to maintain a healthy body. When the muscle is not strengthened, the body becomes weak and flabby. Fortunately for us, Paul in his letter to the Galatians gave us a detailed list of the pounds we should be carrying as believers (Galatians 5:22-23).

He lists these as the fruit of the Spirit. We can think of these as dumbbells. As new believers we may carry these in small increments of two-pound weights. As our love and knowledge for Christ grows, so will our weight bearing of this fruit of the Spirit. Just as our physical body strengthens with free weights, so does our spiritual being with the fruit of the Spirit. The heavier the weights we pump, the more evidence of our spiritual health will develop.

Let's take time to understand each of these weights we are to lift daily:

1) Love

    a)   Read 1 Corinthians 13:4-6. What areas of love are missing from today's society that, if implemented, would create a Love Revolution?

    b)   What is the commandment given to the New Testament believers? (John 15:12-17)

    c)   How can we be an imitator of God? (Ephesians 5:1-2)

2) Joy

    a)   What is the kingdom of God? (Romans 14:17)

    b)   How can we abound in hope by the power of the Holy Spirit? (Romans 15:13)

    c)   What is our strength? (Nehemiah 8:10)

3) **Peace**

a) Define our peace as believers according to
Ephesians 2:14-18.

b) How can this peace help us today? (Philippians 4:7)

4) Longsuffering

a) What are some good examples of longsuffering?
(1 Timothy 1:16; 1 Peter 3:20)

b) Is longsuffering a part of our walk with Christ?
(Ephesians 4:2; Colossians 1:11)

5) Kindness

    a)   When the virtuous woman opens her mouth, what is on her tongue? (Proverbs 31:26)

    b)   Why is it necessary that we be kind to others? (Ephesians 4:32)

6) Goodness

a)   What will follow us if we dwell in the house of the Lord? (Psalm 23:6)

b)   When we walk in the way of goodness, what path will we be on? (Proverbs 2:20)

7) Faithfulness

a)   What did David declare every night? (Psalm 92:2)

b)   To those who say, "God, you are my Father and salvation," what is with them (Psalms 89:24)? Will it ever fail? (Psalm 89:33)

8) Gentleness

a) Who are we to be gentle to? (2 Timothy 2:24; Titus 3:2)

b) What is the definition of "incorruptible beauty"? (1 Peter 3:4)

9) Self-Control

    a)   What is the sequence of events that leads to a full knowledge of Jesus Christ? (2 Peter 1:5-9)

    b)   How can we control our flesh by walking in self-control? (2 Corinthians 10:3-6)

LIFE EXERCISED

I have found that in my life's journey there are different seasons that will bear different fruit. I'm sure, ladies, you can relate when I say there can be days you experience every fruit in a few hours. One of those days for me was the time I totaled my SUV. I had a great, productive day at home. I walked in bearing self-control: cleaning, cooking, and picking up the kids from school. After I picked up the fourth child at the second school, I began to make a left-hand turn, and I experienced a front-end collision that totaled my Ford Expedition.

I saw kindness, love, and gentleness in action as the fireman held each one of my children and laid them on stretchers. I saw the faithfulness and goodness of my heavenly Father when every child was accounted for. There was plenty of smoke—yet no flames. I began to "long suffer" when the police were questioning me: Did you have any alcohol? Were you talking on the phone? Were you listening to the radio? My answer was the same for all three: no.

They took my middle son, Justin, in the helicopter to a trauma center where he spent six days. The rest of us were examined with cuts, bruises, and fractures and sent home. In a few weeks, I once again experienced the faithfulness of God as Justin got the report: his lacerated spleen, fractured sternum, broken pelvis, bruised lung, and torn ligaments in his neck were completely healed. To God be the glory.

LIFTING WEIGHT #2

STRENGTH AND COURAGE

Strength and courage—a powerful dual—would be another constructive weight to bench-press every day. Fifty times in the Bible (NKJV), it reminds us "do not be afraid." Also, in 2 Chronicles 32:6-7, the Word adds that the reciprocal of being afraid is to be "strong and courageous."

As we strengthen our spiritual man and raise our spiritual temperature, we have to develop the confidence that through Christ, even the gates of hell will not prevail against us (Matthew 16:18). God has not given us a spirit of fear (2 Timothy 1:7).

When we exercise with apprehension, we are limiting our bodies from receiving the full effects of the workout. We become timid, slow, and weak. This would not raise our heartbeat as an effectual exercise. Instead, it would only create stress. The same is true for our spiritual being. Yet, when we understand our strength in Christ and walk in godly courage, it propels us into receiving all that God has for us.

THINGS TO CONSIDER

Exactly how strong and courageous are we to be according to God's Word?

1) Is God with us today as He was with Moses? How should we live and what are we to do? (Joshua 1:5-9)

2) What is the heritage of the servant of the Lord? Should we be afraid? (Isaiah 54:17)

3) According to Matthew 11:12-15, how is the kingdom of heaven taken? Does this require strength and courage? Who are others that have carried this same principle?

4) As a believer following Christ, what do we have authority over? Knowing this, does this give you strength and courage? (Luke 10:19)

LIFE EXERCISED

Talk about afraid! I put an ad in the local newspaper to sell our recliner. This man came to my house to buy it and began telling me of his recent release from jail and how society did not trust him. I felt fear well up in my heart and my throat went dry as I began praying under my breath—I was with my preschool son.

The man loaded the recliner on the roof of his very small car. I wondered if he had any intention of really buying it. As the buyer got in his car, my son, J. T., asked, "Who was that man with you?" I said, "What man? The buyer?" to which J. T. responded, "No, the man who left and walked over there. He was here standing by you."

I told J. T. it must have been an angel. I had prayed, and even though I did not see anyone, I believe God used my son to tell me I had no reason to be afraid.

LIFTING WEIGHT #3

HOLINESS

Holiness. This is the part of the exercise where the rubber meets the road. To exercise with holiness is to reach the full potential of the workout. What many people do not realize is that holiness is an absolute necessity to raising our spiritual temperature. Both the Old and New Testaments command believers with the same phrase: "be ye holy" (Leviticus 11:44; 1 Peter 1:15-16 KJV).

Holiness is the mirror image of God. Any gym you may join will have mirrors covering the walls from corner to corner. This can be intimidating at first. Every angle of your body is reflected on the wall for the entire gym to see. The mirrors are to enhance your workout. You can focus on your form, your stance, and your speed in every exercise you perform.

When you begin your repetitions of an exercise, you realize how important it is to stay focused on the mirror. As you watch the mirror, the exercise becomes easier because you can be confident that you are following your coach's instructions.

So it is with our Christian walk. Fortunately, our mirror is not ourselves. Our mirror is God Almighty. The more holiness we apply in our life, the more of God's glory we reflect (2 Corinthians 3:18). At first the idea of being in the presence of a holy God can be intimidating. We need to remember as children of God that we are new creatures in

Christ, and our heavenly Father waits patiently to embrace us (2 Corinthians 5:17). As we exercise with holiness, we will reflect more and more of our Father's glory.

Let's see what the Word says about holiness so that we ourselves can be transformed into His image.

1) What is our reasonable service to God? (Romans 12:1-2)

2) How do we exercise true righteousness and holiness? (Romans 6:19; Ephesians 4:20-24)

3) What should not be in our reputation, when we walk in holiness? (Ephesians 5:3-7)

4) What did God ask the Israelites to write on all their material possessions? What does this tell us about purging our homes? (Zechariah 14:20-21)

5) What are we to pursue so that we can see the Lord? (Hebrews 12:14)

6) According to 2 Corinthians 3:18, can we reflect the image of God?

7) What is being said and done to our Lord God Almighty continually day and night? (Revelation 4:8-11)

8) Knowing this, how important is it that we exercise holiness?

LIFE EXERCISED

This is my heart cry: to be a reflection of my Lord and Savior. I've learned through experience that the only advice worth saying is advice that comes straight from the Word of God. When I first began mentoring to women, I'd spend hours reliving every detail of their experience as we tried to work through it. Wow, those ladies had to sift through a lot of hot air before they were able to receive the advice I gave them. I love you, ladies!

Now I have learned to give advice straight from God's Word, whether it is a verse or a parable. To walk in true holiness we need to speak *His* words not our own.

LIFTING WEIGHT #4

WISDOM AND DISCERNMENT

Dropping the unwanted weight and adding the lean weight requires wisdom and discernment. One of the most concerning verses in the Bible is Hosea 4:6, which says, "*My people* are destroyed for the lack of knowledge." Notice that the Lord is speaking of *His* people. These are the people who are already exercising as believers, yet their demise is their own self.

You see this happen many times with people working out their physical bodies. People can take a power walk or jog with an old pair of tennis shoes and actually hurt their feet instead of strengthening their bodies. The most common exercise mistake is the failure to stretch before and after a workout. Many people have jumped into an exercise routine working out to their full potential, doing many repetitions without taking the time to stretch. Later, they feel the effects of achy, cramping, painful muscles.

What is at fault here? Is it the exercise itself or the lack of knowledge of the importance of stretching? Unfortunately, many give up at this point and never return to their exercise. Yet, a few minutes before and after the workout would have changed their results drastically.

Jesus explained this using an example called "the parable of the sower" (Matthew 13:18-23). In verse 19, Jesus says there will be those people who hear the Word but do not understand it, and the wicked one will steal it from them. Yet in verse 23, Jesus says he who hears the Word and understands it bears fruit. This is why part of our daily exercise routine is lifting wisdom and discernment.

THINGS TO CONSIDER

1) Read Proverbs 2:1-15.

    a) How are we to seek after wisdom and discernment?

    b) What will we understand, when doing so?

c) What does God give to those who walk uprightly?

d) What does wisdom and discernment deliver us from? (verses 10-15)

2) How can we use wisdom with our words and have discernment over our mouth? (Ecclesiastes 5:1-6)

3) Discerning people follow what path? (Hosea 14:9)

4) What is the beginning of wisdom? (Psalm 111:10; Proverbs 1:7; 9:10; Isaiah 33:6)

5) What happens to the woman who applies this to her life? (Proverbs 31:30)

LIFE EXERCISED

Okay, I admit I have overexerted myself many times working out. I jump into an exercise determined to complete it whether my body is ready for it or not. The adrenaline kicks in and wisdom disappears. It is always two days later that the fatigue and pain begin. I spend the rest of the week stretching and kicking myself for not using wisdom. Take it from me, ladies, it's hard to get fit when you hurt yourself so badly you can't move and grow.

I'm grateful that God gives us wisdom and discernment about the silly things, like over-exercising, but He also gives wisdom and discernment generously whenever it is needed. (James 1:5) As a woman, you reach a certain age where everything, head to toe has to be checked. It's wise to routinely have a physical examination. I had completed my routine exam and returned home when I received a phone call from the doctor's office that they wanted to see me immediately. Something was wrong on my X-ray. From that moment on my life became a blur. I remember going from doctor office to doctor office and hospital to hospital for second opinions. It was apparent to these professionals that this disease was indeed in my body. I felt like a lifeless shell going through the motions.

Why now? James and I were finally reaching another season in our married life. My oldest, Jessica, was going away for college and my second oldest, J.T., was planning to attend the University of Nations in Hawaii. Life was good and exciting. How could this be happening? I prayed, searched the scriptures, and asked for wisdom and discernment. I remembered how Mary the mother of Jesus, pondered everything the angel had said in her heart. I discerned in my heart that I too was to ponder this doctor's report. I knew that if I shared this bad news with my children, they would immediately drop all their plans for their futures, to care for me. I shared it only with my husband. I knew that the enemy meant this for evil, but God would turn it around for my good.

Let me tell you, it was hard, not lashing out in my flesh. I wanted the world to feel sorry for me, especially when people would say "Oh, you don't understand" or "You have it so good". I wanted to set them down and explain reality to them. Then that still small suggestion would come to my thoughts, "Trust me". The doctor showed me my X-ray and how it matched the picture in the brochure of the disease spreading through my veins. I confidently told the X-ray technician that I'm sure I do not have that disease.

She walked around the machine and said to me, "Mrs. Carpenter, this is serious; this is abnormal like nothing we've ever seen in you before." My doctor found the top surgeon in our state and scheduled my first surgery before treatment. Was I crying out to God? Absolutely! A few days before the surgery, a sweet grandmother I had met through ministry called. I broke down and shared what I was facing, and the fact my husband was unable to come with me. She immediately said she was going to go with me and stay in that waiting room, praying, no matter how long it took.

When the doctor's office called with the pre-surgery procedures, they mentioned that I was welcome to bring a favorite CD. (Why they don't want you to wear deodorant is beyond me.) At first I brushed it off, but then I couldn't forget about the CD, I prayed, " Lord, would this glorify You?" I took out my box of CDs and asked God to give me wisdom in choosing one. I first searched for a seeker friendly CD, something that may mention God but not be too preachy. I was quickly convicted. I remembered the verse in Matt 10:32, If I confess Jesus before men; then Jesus will confess me before His Father in heaven. If I ever needed my name to be confessed before my Heavenly Father it was now. My eyes fell upon John Waller's CD, *As For Me and My House*. A peace rushed over my body. I knew this was the CD to bring. The next day, I was prepped for surgery and my adopted godly grandmother was in the waiting room praying. The nurse asked for my CD. She didn't give me a headset; instead she played the CD through the entire sound system. It began playing *Our God Reigns Here* and continued with song after song about God's power and redemption story. It played over and over, loud and clear. I kept praying for God's glory to be known and that His righteous may not be forsaken.

I don't even know how many hours went by. Finally, the surgeon sent me to another room for more X-rays. I returned and once more I lay on the operating table. The surgeon gave me a robe and asked me to sit up. As I'm rose up, I noticed, one by one the nurses lined up in the room and just stood there. The surgeon said to me, "I asked for all the nurses to come in to hear what I'm about to say.... You came here and glorified your God.

God showed up and has done a mighty work here today. The disease is gone." She handed me a pink carnation and released me to go home.

"Praise God! Really? I don't have to do anything? Are you sure?"

The doctor was confident and put me on a 6-month re-examine schedule, which lasted only a few years. I'm so grateful that I listened to the wisdom and discernment I received from the Lord at the very beginning. If I had been unwise and shattered my children's dreams, felt sorry for myself and called others about my misfortune, I don't think I would have had the faith to believe God for my miracle. As for the sweet godly grandmother, she was still praying in the waiting room when I was released.

"Hallelujah! To God be all the glory!" ....shouted two tearful women in the parking lot.

VITAMIN VERSES A-Z

Here is an exercise you can complete by choosing verses to inspire your workout. Take daily.

Vitamin A: Affectionate

"Be kindly affectionate to one another with brotherly love, in honor giving preference to one another; not lagging in diligence, fervent in spirit, serving the Lord; rejoicing in hope, patient in tribulation, continuing steadfastly in prayer; distributing to the needs of the saints, given to hospitality." (Romans 12:10-13)

_____

_____

_____

_____

Vitamin B: Broken Spirit

"The sacrifices of God are a broken spirit, a broken and a contrite heart. These, O God, You will not despise." (Psalm 51:17)

_____

_____

_____

_____

_____

Vitamin C: Courageous

"Only be strong and very courageous, that you may observe to do according to all the law which Moses My servant commanded you; do not turn from it to the right hand or to the left, that you may prosper wherever you go." (Joshua 1:7-8)

_____

_____

_____

_____

_____

Vitamin D: Discernment

"He who keeps his command will experience nothing harmful; and a wise man's heart discerns both time and judgment." (Ecclesiastes 8:5)

_____

_____

_____

_____

_____

Vitamin E: Earnest

"Therefore we must give the more earnest heed to the things we have heard, lest we drift away." (Hebrews 2:2)

_____

_____

_____

_____

_____

Vitamin F: Faithful

"His lord said to him, 'Well done, good and faithful servant; you were faithful over a few things, I will make you ruler over many things. Enter into the joy of your lord.'" (Matthew 25:20-22)

_____

_____

_____

_____

Vitamin G: Generous

"Remember this—a farmer who plants only a few seeds will get a small crop. But the one who plants generously will get a generous crop. You must each make up your own mind as to how much you should give. Don't give reluctantly or in response to pressure. For God loves the person who gives cheerfully. And God will generously provide all you need. Then you will always have everything you need and plenty left over to share with others." (2 Corinthians 9:6-8 NLT)

_____

_____

_____

_____

Vitamin H: Holy

"But as he which hath called you is holy, so be ye holy in all manner of conversation; Because it is written, Be ye holy; for I am holy. (1 Peter 1:15-16 KJV)

_____

_____

_____

_____

_____

Vitamin I: Image

"For whom He foreknew, He also predestined to be conformed to the image of His Son, that He might be the firstborn among many brethren." (Romans 8:29)

_____

_____

_____

_____

_____

Vitamin J: Just

"The curse of the LORD is on the house of the wicked, But He blesses the home of the just." (Proverbs 3:33)

_____

_____

_____

_____

_____

Vitamin K: Kind

"And be kind to one another, tenderhearted, forgiving one another, even as God in Christ forgave you." (Ephesians 4:32)

_____

_____

_____

_____

_____

Vitamin L: Lion

"The wicked flee when no one pursues, But the righteous are bold as a lion." (Proverbs 28:1)

_____

_____

_____

_____

_____

Vitamin M: Merciful

"Blessed are the merciful, For they shall obtain mercy." (Matthew 5:7)

_____

_____

_____

_____

_____

Vitamin N: Noble

"These were more noble than those in Thessalonica, in that they received the word with all readiness of mind, and searched the scriptures daily, whether those things were so." (Acts 17:11 KJV)

_____

_____

_____

_____

Vitamin O: Ordained

"Ye have not chosen me, but I have chosen you, and ordained you, that ye should go and bring forth fruit, and that your fruit should remain: that whatsoever ye shall ask of the Father in my name, he may give it you." (John 15:16 KJV)

_____

_____

_____

_____

_____

Vitamin P: Peaceable

"Finally, brethren, farewell. Become complete. Be of good comfort, be of one mind, live in peace; and the God of love and peace will be with you." (2 Corinthians 13:11)

_____

_____

_____

_____

_____

Vitamin Q: Quiet

"And that ye study to be quiet, and to do your own business, and to work with your own hands, as we commanded you." (1 Thessalonians 4:11 KJV)

_____

_____

_____

_____

_____

Vitamin R: Righteous

"The mouth of the righteous is a well of life, But violence covers the mouth of the wicked." (Proverbs 10:11)

_____

_____

_____

_____

_____

Vitamin S: Strength

"Have I not commanded you? Be strong and of good courage; do not be afraid, nor be dismayed, for the LORD your God is with you wherever you go." (Joshua 1:9)

_____

_____

_____

_____

_____

Vitamin T: Truth

"For I rejoiced greatly when brethren came and testified of the truth that is in you, just as you walk in the truth. I have no greater joy than to hear that my children walk in truth." (3 John 3-4)

_____

_____

_____

_____

Vitamin U: Unmoveable

"Therefore, my beloved brethren, be ye steadfast, unmovable, always abounding in the work of the Lord, forasmuch as ye know that your labor is not in vain in the Lord." (1 Corinthians 15:58 KJV)

_____

_____

_____

_____

_____

Vitamin V: Vision

"Where there is no vision, the people perish: but he that keepeth the law, happy is he." (Proverbs 29:18 KJV)

_____

_____

_____

_____

_____

Vitamin W: Wisdom

"Behold, I send you out as sheep in the midst of wolves. Therefore be wise as serpents and harmless as doves." (Matthew 10:16-17)

_____

_____

_____

_____

_____

Vitamin X: X marks the spot

"I press toward the mark for the prize of the high calling of God in Christ Jesus." (Philippians 3:14 KJV)

_____

_____

_____

_____

_____

Vitamin Y: Yielded

"Neither yield ye your members as instruments of unrighteousness unto sin: but yield yourselves unto God, as those that are alive from the dead, and your members as instruments of righteousness unto God." (Romans 6:13 KJV)

_____

_____

_____

_____

_____

Vitamin Z: Zealous

"Do not let your heart envy sinners, But be zealous for the fear of the LORD all the day." (Proverbs 23:17)

_____

_____

_____

_____

_____

ABOUT THE AUTHOR

The author, Tammy Carpenter resides in the countryside of Delaware on her husband's family farm. This is where Tammy has found her highest calling, being a wife to James for over twenty-one years, and a mother to their four children Jessica, James III, Justin and Jeremy.

Tammy began serving the Lord at a very young age. Her childhood salvation birthed in her a passion to lead others to find life in Christ. She had the unique experience of spending 13 years of her childhood being raised at Liberty Bible College in Pensacola, Florida where her father was a student. As a youth, Tammy traveled on Liberty Church's mission team—speaking, singing, and performing dramas. As a high school graduate, she completed Intensive

Christian Training at Last Days Ministry, YWAM—Youth With A Mission. Once married and living in Delaware, Tammy continued her education receiving a degree in human services.

Upon college graduation, she immediately began serving women in her local Pregnancy Care Center, first as a Volunteer Coordinator and then, quickly became a women's counselor and joined their speaker bureau. Her passion to lead others to Christ continued as she served faithfully in church; teaching Sunday School for 17 years, as well as the Vacation Bible School director and Children's Church director. Currently, she is a key part in facilitating ladies Bible studies, serving on the prayer team and church's host team. Community wise Tammy serves locally as a board member for a Pregnancy Care center and as Assistant Teaching Director of CBS. (Community Bible Study)

In pursuing her own intimacy with Christ, it became evident to her that God uses the physical to define the spiritual. Using this concept and a life long weight battle of her own, Tammy shares her realizations in this ladies manual. A resource women can use to walk through the Bible individually or as a group. Her direct approach as an exercise coach opens the eyes and hearts of those studying to the particular essential principles the Lord has given us. Tammy's vision is that as many women as possible will achieve their true, full potential in Christ and live vigorous, purpose-driven lives with spiritual synergy.

The illustrator, Jessica Carpenter, has an associate of arts degree from the University of Delaware. She resides in

West Palm Beach, Florida, where she is currently enrolled at Palm Beach Atlantic University and working towards her bachelor's degree in graphic design and ministry. As a child, Jessica gave her heart to the Lord, and through the years she has expressed herself with art. As a teen, she attended Sussex Technical High School where she received distinguished certification in her graphic design technical area. Jessica hopes to use her talent to further the gospel and ministry of our Lord Jesus Christ.

To contact:

Tammy: e-mail jlctrc92@aol.com
Facebook: Spiritual Synergy

Jessica: e-mail jrenee@udel.edu

ACKNOWLEDGMENTS

My deepest appreciation to . . .

Jessica Carpenter—I'm grateful for your time and dedication to completing these illustrations. You have blessed me in becoming a woman of integrity with a heart to heal the brokenhearted. May God's anointing flow through you freely in everything that you say and do.

Verna Clemmer, author of *The Caregiver's Journal*—Thank you for the decades of love you and your family have given me. I am appreciative of your thoughtfulness in editing and fine-tuning this Bible study. Your gentle spirit and prayers inspired me through completion. May God richly reward you as His faithful servant.

Terry Bolick—My unofficial manager/guardian angel. I'm extremely grateful for your constant prayer support, Biblical guidance, and encouragement to further God's kingdom. May God's hand extend to you a full reward for your selfless acts of kindness.

Prayer partners—What a blessing you have been to me. My dear friends stretch from nearby to over state lines and across continents, yet our prayers have tied us together eternally. Each one of you has paved the way for this study to be birthed. May you receive a hundredfold blessing for this harvest.

Ladies—Thank you to the many women who have shared with me their stories, whether it was through a Bible study, phone call, e-mail, appointment, lunch, coffee, or the like. It is your vulnerability that has given me the courage to print this book. Thank you for your story, and may God Himself touch you in an unforeseen way.

James Carpenter Jr.—To my husband whom I've loved for twenty-one years, thank you for your faithfulness to our four children and me. Your dedication to your core values in Christ is a wealth of security to me. May God continue to bless you in everything you put your hands to.

James III (J.T.), Justin, Jeremy—To the men God has entrusted to me as sons. I'm continually blessed by your spirits and the men of integrity that you each have become. You've brought me much joy, and I'm truly grateful for the many belly laughs that we continue to have. May you each be blessed with power and might from our almighty God in everything that you say and do.

STUDY HELPS

Study to shew thyself approved unto God, a
workman that needeth not to be ashamed,
rightly dividing the word of truth.
(2 Timothy 2:15 KJV)

This manual may be completed individually or as a group.
The answers to each question can be found in the Bible
verse after the question.

Individually

- Pray each time you begin a chapter. Invite the Holy
  Spirit to lead, guide, and counsel you.
- Look up each verse listed in both the study and
  the questions. Study the biblical stories listed and
  discover how they apply to your life today.
- Use a dictionary for any word that needs to be
  defined.
- Keep a teachable attitude.

Group

- Pray for the Holy Spirit's guidance before each study.
- Encourage local exercise groups to study along with
  you.
- Group leaders may incorporate their own testimonies
  that go along with the chapter. Group members
  may want to share their own experiences.

- Keep it humble. Do not allow a platform for the extremist. If the group gets "off topic," gently guide them back to the study.
- Dig into each Bible story. Talk specifically how these stories influence us as women today.
- Allow everyone to speak in the group. Everyone's input is important.
- Invite women to share only their own stories, testimonies, and prayer requests. Any comment other than that of their own experience needs to be shared only with permission from that person.
- The "Life Exercised" paragraphs are intended to inspire you in sharing your own life's story.
- Encourage, encourage, encourage!

CPSIA information can be obtained at www.ICGtesting.com
Printed in the USA
BVOW01s1200230816

459908BV00001B/10/P

9 781490 898230